The Center for Contemplative Practice
shares

MINING FOR HEAVENLY GOLD WHILE ON EARTH

HOW TO CENTER YOURSELF ON WHAT IS AUTHENTIC

Michael F. Conrad, Ed.D.

This edition was produced for Print-on-Demand
distribution by The Center for Contemplative

The Center for Contemplative Practice
2402 Glenshire Lane, Tallahassee, FL 32309

Printed in the United States of America
September, 2016

All references to Scripture come from the
New Jerusalem Bible, Doubleday Broadway, Inc.

Table of Contents

"The most difficult part of life is seeing what is underneath your feet. Like the story, Acres of Diamonds, tantalizingly told by Earl Nightingale, you have all the help you need to get you to Heaven. You were not made to live Forever on earth. That is just a place to learn how to live authentically. You care destined for another complete dimension, one for which you are not prepared, unless you know where to look, and how to get ready. Your church, mosque or synagogue can help you prepare for the trip to...Forever. If you do not believe in a religion, fall back on spirituality, which helps you to gain the perspective that life is worth living. First, you must choose a center that will make the jump from matter to pure energy."

Michael F. Conrad, Ed.D

WHY READ THIS BOOK?

Spiritual books are such a rich venue for expanding your spiritual universe. This book is a quick read to allow you to think about your center and what is authentic about your life. The book provides you with the opportunity to write down your thoughts about specific questions. The product is yours. Spirituality, in its most generic form (the 500,000 foot level) asks three questions. If you answer these three questions, you will discover your center, what is authentic about it, and analyze if it will get you to Heaven.

Before you die, three questions you must answer are:

1. Who are you? What is your center? Because you are human, you must struggle throughout your whole life to keep yourself centered. Read my book, Three Rules of the Spiritual Universe, to read more about how struggling with your center is part of the price you pay for freely choosing an authentic center. Centers do not automatically stay that way. Each day, you must struggle to keep yourself centered on what is right and true. I can not tell you what an authentic center is, but I can provide a process to find it. This is NOT the centering prayer method.

2. What is your destiny? Where are you headed? Choosing the correct center is the most important aspect of free will, and may be the reason you have the ability to reason. We have reason for a reason. The purpose of this life is about preparing for the next level of existence.

3. How can you get there from here? Every day, in every way, you are tempted to substitute God's will with that of your own. You have help to keep you on the straight and narrow. Once you know where your direction, you spend your whole life preparing for the trip. Churches, if they are authentic, will help you prepare your mind, your heart, and your spirit to live... Forever. You may have to die alone, but, ironically, you must prepare to live…Forever through relationships.

HOW TO USE THIS WORKBOOK EFFECTIVELY.

This is a book, a quick read that gives you a chance to think about some topics. YOU are the most important part of this book. Any book is only as effective as you want it to be. This is a tool for you to use. It is meant to help you think critically about where you are in your life, where you want to be, and some strategies to get there. You will do all the hard work. The book will just help you to shape your thoughts towards a productive conclusion.

This is a book designed for you to read, but also to use with your adult learning programs. Do the exercises in this book with others you trust. This is a perfect tool to help you start an adult spiritual directions center.

This is a book about how to center yourself. You will have space to write your thoughts about specific questions concerning your spirituality. At the outside edge of each page is space to write any notes you might have about what you read.

Take time to look up the Scriptural references in the New Jerusalem Bible, Doubleday. You can read it online at: http://www.kofc. duq.edu/scripture/

Create a peaceful place, a containment field, where you can go to process your thoughts. It could be a quiet seashore, a beautiful garden with fragrant flowers, an apple orchard with rows of blossoming flowers. Imagine yourself in this place of refreshment, where there are no interruptions, no problems and no issues to confront. Even if you do this exercise in a group, it is just you and your spiritual world.

Ten Spiritual Ideas

Before you begin reading about centering, here are some ideas you might find interesting.

1. Centering yourself without asking your spouse, and maybe even your children, could be short-sighted. Your direction, after all, is not yours alone to make. Your family should also identify their spiritual centers. When you discuss these various centers, a pattern should emerge. No one travels through this life alone.

2. The answers you give are not cast in stone…Forever. Life changes. Priorities pop up. At least you have the framework to keep making all things new, if you chose an unauthentic center. This centering is not the same as centering prayer.

3. Use the centering process as a learning experience. Put your ego aside. These questions will help you and your loved ones to talk about topics you may rarely have had the opportunity to discuss. You may never get around to it. Do it now!

4. Your past is not your present, but it will influence your future. A person who has lived any significant amount of time knows that forgiveness and repentance is the super glue that re-sticks those things we knock loose in our lives. Read Matthew 18:21-22. We humans never learn, we keep repeating our mistakes over and over, even when we know better. What does this mean about being human? About

5. Your Center should determine the North on your life's compass. A funny thing about Centers; you can lose them, if you are not careful. You need the context of your church to test your behavior against the practices that The Master left us.

6. Every time you pray for humility and enlightenment, you re-audit yourself. Humility means that God is your Center and you measure all things against Love itself.

7. When you die, you die alone, but when you enter Heaven, you must do so in the company of The Master, the Apostles, and your loved ones waiting there to greet you. If you believe this, then the rest of your life will be devoted to packing for the trip, be you a teen or an elder.

8. What you pack for the trip to Heaven, you can take with you. Remember that Heaven is God's playground and you are invited as an honored adopted son or daughter. When you take the self-audit, and are asked about "Whom You Want to Become", remember that what you treasure in life and link to God's will, will be your Heaven later on. Plan carefully but joyfully!

9. Not everything you want to achieve is achievable. If you are 80 years of age and want to be a brain surgeon, it is clear you will not achieve that goal. If you are 80 years of age and want to read to youngsters who need brain surgery, that is do-able. Remember, you are packing for the trip to...Forever.

10. Whose side are you on? When his Secretary of War stated to Abraham Lincoln that he thought they would win the Civil War because God was on their side, Lincoln uttered the famous quote, " I would much rather think it is better to be on God's side, than to think He is on our side." When you read this book, do so with the proper perspective. Life is about discovering God's treasures so that we can live with them now, then take those riches to Heaven with us.

WHAT IS YOUR CENTER?

"As you center goes, so you go. Be careful what you select as your center. That is your god. Centers should be based on principles. Principles come from your denominational point of view. Denominations have a center that comes from religion. Religions have a center that comes from spirituality. The difficulty is, all of these must align, if you truly and authentically fulfill your destiny." Michael F. Conrad, Ed.D.

Note: This concept of Centering is not Centering Prayer. They are separate methodologies and purposes, both good and appropriate.

WHAT IS YOUR CENTER? Before you begin to think about your center, look at the BIG PICTURE. What is the one center you have that all others depend upon. It is called a principle because, like the foundation of a house, it is the based upon which all other values are built. This next section will enable you to select your center.

WHERE DOES SPIRITUALITY FIT? This Lazer book is for those who consider themselves spiritual. It will not direct you to one religion, but it will ask you to think about your relationships with God, your family, your friends, and your personal ministry to and with others. To be authentic, your spirituality, religion, denomination, and personal belief must be aligned with what is true. You must align yourself against the center you choose. What you choose is your god, so make it a good one. You have free choice to be able to choose what you want as your center. Your (eternal) life depends on it. Below is a diagram of how it all fits together. Do you agree with this view of reality? If not, how would you draw how spirituality fits, in your world view?

THE COLLECTIVE PICTURE OF HUMANITY

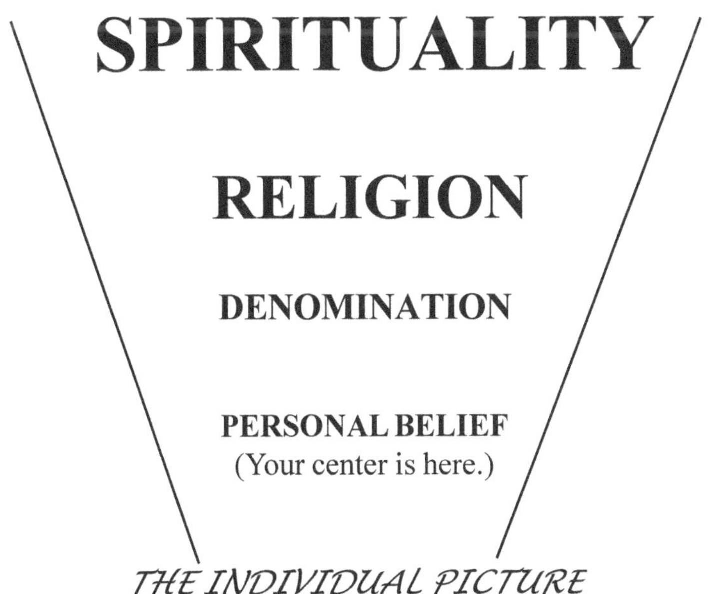

THE INDIVIDUAL PICTURE

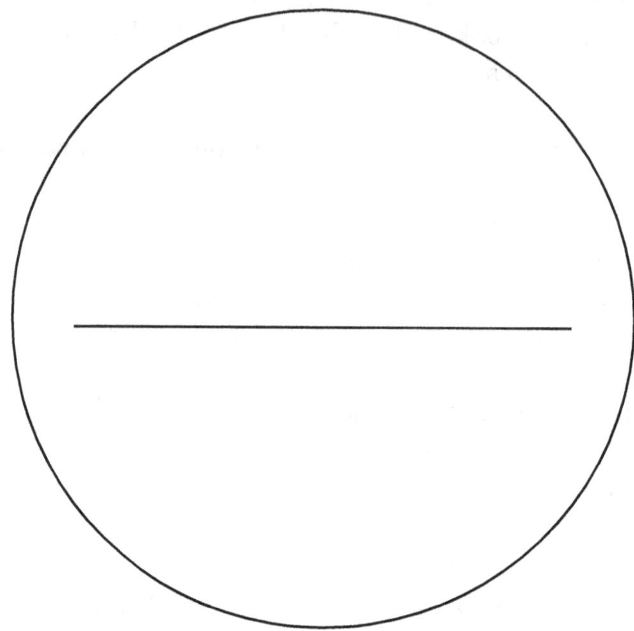

What is the one principle that, if everything else was taken away, would be the core of your life? What is your ground floor? What is the bull's-eye, or core center of your life? Inside the circle above, write down one or two words that describe this center. You may wish to use a short scripture quote. If your center is more than a mere slogan, you will put it on your bathroom mirror and look at it every morning.

Treat each page of the following Lazer book spiritual reading as a separate thought it should be a thought starter, and you may not agree with what is said. Keep on reading! Let these ideas challenge and stimulate your thoughts.

Your spirit does not grow by repeating old thoughts, but by creating new ones and relating them to life situations. Read Luke 5:37.

> *If the center of your life is your spouse, your children, your mother or father, you have a problem.*

1. That statement sounds heartless, don't you think? Let us think critically. If you did place your loved ones at the center of your life, and, hypothetically, they all died in a plane crash, with what would you be left? Your center is who you are.

2. The Master said: *"If any man comes to me without hating his father, mother, wife, children, brothers, sisters, and yes, his own life too, he cannot be my disciple."* Luke 14:26-27

3. I have always had a problem with that Scripture. When you look at the Master's quote in terms of the first value you must place at your center, what he says makes complete sense. Do not put humans or things at your center. Do not put yourself at the center of your life. When you put family, friends, and spouse at your center, they fade away, just like old soldiers. They become as outdated as a 286 MHz computer, or a Black & White television set. Humans make poor terrible centers. You must select a center that has energy, durability, and consistency. Any ideas?

> *Here comes the kicker.*
> *You, and only you, can place a person, thing, or an idea at your center.*

1. What you discover about the meaning of life and what is CRITICALLY important, you can place at your very center. It is the principle from which all other activities flow in any way. It is your core. The core is the foundation stone of your values.

2. One of the things that separate us from the monkeys is our ability to choose a center. We can select any value we want for that center. Some of us choose a false center, some choose wisely, while some just cannot be bothered.

3. How do you know what center is correct? Is it fame, money, adulation, sex, drugs, booze, religion, family, spouse, or work? The meaning of life for you is what you choose for your center. You alone can call the shots. That is the ultimate free choice. You can only have one center.

4. Your center may make you uncomfortable. Why? Perhaps it is due to the constant stress between your animal self (doing what I want) and your spiritual self (doing what God wants of me).

5. A center should be something or someone who lasts...Forever.

ARE THESE CENTERS WORTH LIVING?

FALSE CENTERS

Drugs, Sex, Alcohol

These centers make you feel good for now. Where will you be in a hundred years, if you have the centers in the box above?

You are free to select drugs, orgiastic sex, and alcohol as your center. Eric Fromm in his book, *The Art of Loving*, calls these three centers "unauthentic" because they do not get at what it means to be human. *http://en.wikipedia.org/wiki/Eric_fromm* Think critically! Part of Fromm I use to explain what separates being authentically human from someone who is not. You may disagree with this.

You will not learn the art of loving by turning to these false centers. These are the "feel good" centers. Using one of these centers is like eating cotton candy--it tastes good but there is no substance, no nutrition, and no meaning. Put any of these false centers at your core and you will never find the meaning of why you are here on earth. These three center only take from you, they can never give you what you need to be more human. Can you imagine living your whole life with these three centers as your core? How boring! How destructive! These centers will not al- low you to reach your destiny as a human being. They do not sustain values, but merely destroy them. Yet, many of us choose the "feel good" centers because they offer less pain and more pleasure. How about you?

Here is a sacred cow that needs to be milked. I am not against religion, but I am cautioning you against making religion your center. Why do I say that?

Religion can never be a good center. It is the guide for the journey, but it can never be the journey itself. Once you put religion at your center, you may look at all other centers as being false. After all, you have the truth, so, other centers may be wrong. Wonder if you do not like what your minister says. Are you going to leave that church for one more reasonable? This is musical churches, named after the famous game, musical chairs. Humans have been playing this game for centuries.

A center is a principle that does not change. It is truth. It is the meaning of your life. It is the reason why humans are the only intelligent beings in the universe, as far as we know. Where you find truth is one of the challenges facing you. Religion itself may not provide you with the truth, if it lacks an authentic center. Your center is important because you take that center and all other values with you, to Heaven.

ARE THESE CENTERS WORTH LIVING?

FALSE CENTERS

Money.

When money is your center, everything you do, every value you have, all your energy goes into making money. This is sometimes called a passion or fixation on getting rich. Making money provides you with the basic needs of life, and it is also the way you provide security for yourself in your old age, but it is a terrible center.

In this case, passion has its price. What happens to your life when your world goes bankrupt, or you lose your business? If you use this false center as your core value, your ground, you are standing on gelatin. Do not be surprised if your ground begins to wobble eventually.

Is any of this going to help you when it really counts, i.e., storing up treasures you can take with you to Heaven? If you do not store up spiritual treasures, what will you carry with you to Heaven? Matter does not matter in Heaven. Money makes a very poor choice for a center. You cannot take it with you, money that is. What treasures can you possible carry with you, and how do you transport them through the fourth door of life, the portal to Heaven?

ARE THESE CENTERS WORTH LIVING?

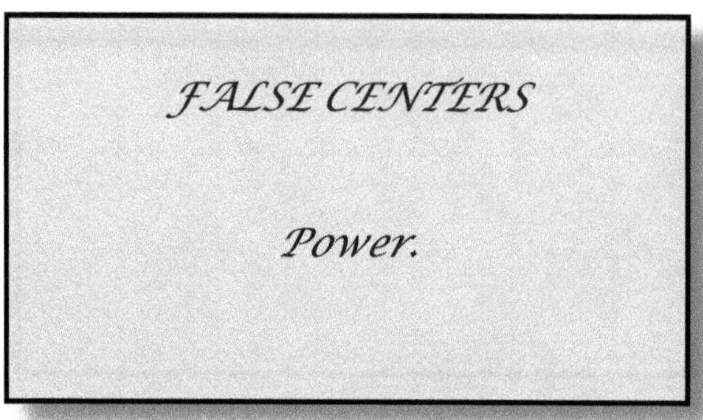

Power is an aphrodisiac. It is a drug that lulls you into thinking that you are as important as you think you are.

Lord Acton said *Power corrupts and absolute power corrupts absolutely.* Wise words. The reason power corrupts is that we begin to believe you are powerful. If power is your center, there is no room for humility. Humility means you recognize that your importance is linked to the worth of others. In the case of a spiritual person, you realize that your worth depends on doing God's will each day. Here are some thoughts:

- Doing God's will is not exactly an exciting prospect. The challenge comes in looking at everyday events through God's eyes and giving him glory and praise.
- You are the eyes and ears, the hands and feet, and the mouth piece for an invisible God.
- Human power is not strong enough to get you to Heaven, if you are against God.
- Hoarding power always subtracts from your worth, rather than adding to it.
- Empowering others always multiplies your power. Seek out power that comes from God.
- In any event, how much human power can you store up and you are satisfied? Never enough, my friend, never enough!

Want to know the power that will get you to Heaven? Read what The Master says in Matthew 20:24-28.

WHY CENTER
YOURSELF?
Matthew 6: 33-34

"Set your hearts on his kingdom first, and on his righteousness, and all these other things will be given you as well. Do not worry about tomorrow; tomorrow will take care of itself. Each day has trouble of its own."

"Centering yourself means you know who you are, where you are going, and how to get there."

The Center for Contemplative Practice

HOW TO CENTER YOURSELF.

HOW TO CENTER YOURSELF

Select a sheet of ordinary writing paper. Tear it into four equal pieces.

On each piece of paper write one value you hold at the core of your value system.

At the very core of who you are is one principle from which all others flow. Think of a principle as the hub of the bicycle wheel. If you place a false center there, your behavior will follow.

Every day, you must center yourself on that center. Every day! Only you can select your center, not your church, not your spouse or children. You alone will be judged on your selection of what is central to your life. Choose wisely!

HOW TO CENTER YOURSELF

> **Of the four pieces of paper in front of you, select the one that is of <u>least</u> value to you.**
>
> **You must select one to discard.**

The difficulty is in selecting which one to discard. Why is one more important than the others?

Take your time. Think about it. Pray about it. Humans do not like to think at this level because it makes them uncomfortable.

HOW TO CENTER YOURSELF

> **Of the three remaining values, select the one that has <u>less value</u> to you than the others.**
>
> **You must select one, even if they are all equal in value.**

Resist the temptation to tell yourself that all of these values are the same.

Think critically! What is the one principle upon which all others rest?

If you were to diagram your life, this would be the foundation stone.

HOW TO CENTER YOURSELF

Study the two remaining values, in silence. Of the two values, select one that is the most important for you, a value you consider to be at the center or core of your spiritual life.

You must select one, even if they are both equal.

The most important value is your final selection. The other three values are also core values. In reality, they are all core values of your life, one of which is the principle of your life. This center is your reason for being. This is your Heaven on earth. This will be your Heaven... Forever. Now comes the hard part. You must keep yourself centered on this principle for the rest of your life. Think this is impossible? It is. That is why there is forgiveness for your sins. Sin means you let your center slip and have replaced it with another one that is false. That is why you need to take up your cross daily. For the rest of your life, God gives you the energy to keep your equilibrium. It takes daily struggle.

Now comes the hard part. All you have to do is keep yourself centered.

ANALYZE YOUR CENTER

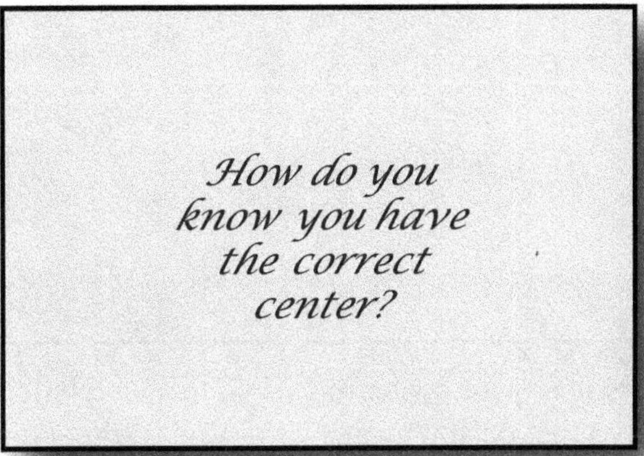

If you want to live in the spiritual universe Forever, there are three questions you should ask yourself.

1. *Is my center a person?*

2. *Is my center going to help me a hundred years from now?*

3. *Does this center help me to fulfill my purpose on earth by knowing, loving, and serving God and others, so that I can be happy in Heaven?*

Are you religious in your belief but not spiritual in your practice? Do you know that the difference makes you different?

You can lead a perfectly fulfilled life on the human level and still not inherit the Kingdom of Heaven. Do you know the reasons why? Think about it!

ANALYZE YOUR CENTER

THE FIRST QUESTION

Is your center a person?

Having a person at your center means you value relationship. Having God as that person means you value spiritual relationship. Early in the development of religious thought, a milestone was reached when the early Hebrews stumbled upon the notion that God was a person.

"When Abram was ninety-nine years old, Yahweh appeared to him and said, 'I am El Shaddai. Bear yourself blameless in my presence, and I will make a Covenant between myself and you, and increase your numbers greatly. I will establish my Covenant between myself and you, and make your descendants after you, generation to generation, a Covenant in perpetuity, to be your God and the God of your descendants after you.'" Genesis 17:1-8

Are you part of this living Covenant with a person, the God of Abraham? Why not? If you are not part of this covenant, you may be missing what God is telling you.

Authentic centers, like life principles, do not change. Select a center that will be there now, and in the future.

ANALYZE YOUR CENTER

THE SECOND QUESTION

Is your center going to help you a hundred years from now?

1. A center that is core to the spiritual universe will sustain you now, and Forever. It is true not because you believe it, but because it is aligned with God's truth.

2. If you placed DRUGS at your center, because you think that is what life is all about, will that center sustain you in a hundred years? Where will you be?

3. Psalm 90 puts it this way:
   "Lord, you have been our refuge age after age. Before the mountains were born,
   before the earth or the world came to birth,
   you were God from all eternity and forever."

4. Will your center protect you and sustain you in Heaven, where there is no matter, no time, no space, only pure energy? If you discover the answer to that question, you will have learned. If your center is a THING, your center is dead. If your center is a person, and that person is God, you are alive...Forever.

ANALYZE YOUR CENTER

THE THIRD QUESTION

Does this center help you to fulfill your purpose on earth by knowing, loving, and serving God, so that you can be happy in Heaven?

Does your center DO anything for you or for others? If you are linked to God, you are a DO-ER, not just a TALK-ER. Knowing the Lord is like saying, you love someone. Without showing that love, you have cotton candy inside. You are all sweetness inside, without any nourishment or value.

If you consider yourself alone in the world, then you may not have the correct center. You are here for a purpose. Your purpose will be different from mine. Your journey will be different than mine. We have the same destiny, but there is only one gate through which all of us must pass to get there -- the Master. Read John 10:7-8. Life is a search for what is meaningful for YOU. You are born alone, you live alone, and you will die alone. That does not mean you must be lonely. Spirituality means you are looking at life through God's lenses, and you have included God in what you see as meaningful. With God at your center, you are never lonely. You find your purpose in life through relationships with others people.

Heaven is God's playground. He makes the rules. You will know the truth and the truth will make you free.

ANALYZE YOUR CENTER

> *Does your center give you the spiritual energy to find meaning on a boring day?*

1. If you are truly lonely, your will be looking for someone to give YOU something. You can be bored easily, because you are waiting to be entertained. You react to life. You fit into life's plan for you.
2. If you are your center, your center will not sustain you, for you are the source of your own power, and we know what kind of power failures we humans have.
3. When you center yourself on the source of all power and energy, you plug into what is most meaningful and why you were created.
4. Knowing that God values you makes you valuable. Do not settle for less than your very best. You are destined to live with God, so start living like it. You are worth the price of redemption, or at least God thought so.
5. You are what you value. Knowing what God values makes you like God. Your center is a value, but one that should give you the power to get to Heaven. Does it?

SALIENT THOUGHTS

Be perfect, as your Heavenly Father is perfect.

Who is as perfect as God, who is 100% of his nature? This nature is pure energy, pure knowledge, and pure love. In fact, we humans could not even grasp what this means, until God sent his only son to us to show us. Read John 3:15-16. We are still trying to figure out what all this means. Today, denominations who follow The Master disagree among themselves as to what this means and how to be perfect. In itself, this shows how imperfect we humans are. We cannot even agree on what the greatest event to happen since creation means. Other religions do not even consider The Master an event at all. What chaos! God wants humans to fulfill their destiny, not as animals who die, but as adopted sons and daughters who share life...Forever. He gave us his only Son to show us how to live in such a way, that we can fulfill our destiny, and be happy forever in Heaven. The Son left us gifts, or tools, to help us confront the major obstacles that would keep us from our intended inheritance. They make up in us with grace that which we lack. They are occasions where we interface with pure energy. They are: reception as an adopted son or daughter, the ability to see what is invisible, a lifestyle that encourages sustained relationship, the ability to re-center ourselves with God and each other, and food for the journey.

If only perfect beings exist in Heaven, how can we get there?

SALIENT THOUGHTS

What does forgiveness have to do with being centered?

In my book, The Three Rules of the Spiritual Universe, rule number two states that, once you have found your center, you will spend the rest of your life trying to keep it there. This life-time struggle only end in Heaven. Humans are simultaneously, strong and weak, fickle and yet so desirous of stability, principled yet prone to sin, spiritual yet so vulnerable to being an animal. It is this tension between the spiritual universe and the mental and physical universes that characterizes the constant struggle to center ourselves in what is authentic. The question is what is it? For those who have accepted that they are the center of their universe, they are the final arbiter of good and evil. God has no part in their decision-making. For those who have accepted a value system outside of themselves, specifically values that come from a Creator, God is the principle against which we find meaning. For those choosing this last way of thinking, we have a chance to get to Heaven. Forgiveness comes into play because no one gets to Heaven unless they are perfect as the Heavenly Father is perfect. So, who would stand a chance? By yourself, no way. With God making up in you that which is lacking, you have a chance, if you can keep your balance. Forgiveness is the critical tool to help you become re-centered on God. Forgiveness is a tool for re-centering yourself on what is important. Forgiveness is a way to align yourself with God's will, God's grace, and God's purpose. Forgiveness means God is number one, family is number two, and you are number three.

SALIENT THOUGHTS

Do you live in the Garden of Eden or the Kingdom of Heaven?

Adam and Eve lived in the Garden of Eden, a mythical place of pure happiness. Because of their desire to be God, they were thrown out of the Garden of Eden, to wander the earth. The Master came to liberate us from wandering in the desert of our sinfulness and to be free to accept our heritage, that which Adam and Eve lost. Read Romans 5:12-21. Our age is far removed from Adam and Eve, yet the effects of that original sin is with us. This tendency to default back to our animal heritage is countered by God's grace, and our faith in what The Master tells us. Spirituality, as I define it, allows us to fulfill our destiny as spiritual apes. Spirituality allows us to enter the Kingdom of Heaven, while on this earth. We learn what it means to be a disciple, we know how all life fits into God's plan, we learn to love unconditionally, and we serve the earth and its people as stewards of justice and truth.

You know you are living in the Garden of Eden when:

- You can see how the fading light of evening reminds you of what awaits you in Heaven;
- You can know the mysteries of how to see with the eyes of faith;
- You can just love others simply because they are there and, when you see them, you see The Father;
- You can serve others unconditionally, despite it causing you inconvenience and some discomfort;
  You can translate the activities of this life with a spiritual view of what is actually important.

SALIENT THOUGHTS

The Kingdom of Heaven is within you.

In Luke 17:28, he speaks of the Kingdom of God being among you. Another translation of this is "within you." The difference seems slight, but significant. Although I am not a biblical expert, I like the latter version better. I like it better because the word "within" means inside you, not outside. To me, The Kingdom of Heaven within you means:

- Heaven begins when you recognize that you are spiritual;
- Heaven begins while you are on earth;
- You create your heaven by aligning yourself with the source of all energy, pure love, pure knowledge, and pure service;
- Heaven is living out with the Master, that which you learned while on earth. Different people have different levels of capacity, depending on how closely they align with The Truth;
- What you discover on earth that is linked to the will of The Father. You can take with you to Heaven;
- On earth, Heaven is making linkages using relationships and discovering what is meaningful;
- On earth, the Kingdom of Heaven begins with you, but is linked with the collective experiences of others (church);
- The church is the collective Kingdom of Heaven on earth, as well as everyone in Heaven, with The Master as Head;
- The frame of reference for your Kingdom of Heaven on earth will be the same parameters you will have after you die. What are the implications of this statement? Is it true?

You must build your frame of reference, Faith only gives you the tools. You can have the seeds of Faith, but if you do not plant and cultivate them, they will not grow, Read Matthew 13.

ANALYZE YOUR CENTER

THE ULTIMATE QUESTION

What is God's center?

1. The center of God is pure energy, pure love, and pure service. Humans do not even have a word for it.
2. We have not a clue what pure energy is because our only measuring sticks are material ones.
   Science measures physical energy, it cannot measure love, much less off the scale, spiritual energy. What
3. The spiritual universe is the only one that allows a human to approach the ultimate question, "Is there reality beyond what I can touch, see, smell, taste, and hear?" You have reason for a reason. You have the ultimate computer, one only one powerful enough to communicate with a Being so far beyond us, that he had to come to earth to give us the User ID and Password.
4. The only way you can know the answer to the ultimate question is that God gave us both the question rom Abraham and Moses, and the ultimate answer from the Master. God's User ID is IAM; God's Password is: LETITBE
5. Look on the next page for the Q&A.

ANALYZE YOUR CENTER

Moses asked:

"Who are you?"

God answered:

"I am the one who is."

****

The Master answered Moses' question more fully:

"I am the way, the truth, and the life."

God's center only makes sense in Heaven. There, pure energy just exists...Forever.

LEARNING POINTS

1. What you put at your center is the very core of what it means to be human.

2. Your purpose is to find the correct center that leads you to the Kingdom of Heaven.

3. Some are content to live their lives in the Garden of Eden, where all their dreams seem to come true, but actually, do not.

4. Humans can be seduced into thinking that the Garden of Eden is the Kingdom of Heaven.

5. Humans have the freedom to choose whatever center they wish. Having a center is not the same as having the correct center. Having the correct center means you must use God's energy and grace to keep you on target.

6. Having a center and keeping it focused are two different challenges. Organized religions serve a useful purpose to help keep us focused on what is true. The process is called daily conversion.

7. You have the greatest computer ever created, one that can open the gates of Heaven. Do you know how to access God's ID and the Password?

WHERE ARE YOU HEADED?

"God talks the spiritual language. You must learn to listen spiritually, if you are to communicate. This workbook may provide you with some tools. Remember, a life plan is one a one-time event, even though you may think you have spent a lot of time writing this down. Spiritual Life Planning last as long as you are alive. All life is a preparation to live...Forever. You must spend a lifetime preparing for the trip, and what a trip it is. God asks, 'Quo Vadis?' or, 'where are you going?' Do you have an answer?"

The Center for

What does your Heaven look like?

Draw four or five circles on a sheet of paper. Look at them. Can you make titles, connections, relationships, with these circles? All life is connected.

If you are spiritual, you have expanded your perspective to include Heaven.

NINE PRINCIPLES OF SPIRITUALITY

Here are some principles of spirituality that are at the core of my thinking. I share them with you in the hopes that they will stimulate your contemplation. Please use your reasoning ability to review them.

1. **Being spiritual is a free act of the will.** You can only be spiritual with an act of the will. It is a matter of choice. What you choose may or may not be spiritual, so be careful.
2. **Your purpose is to find the correct center that leads you to the Kingdom of Heaven.** You have reason for a reason. Not all spiritual leaders will lead you to Heaven. Not all denominations will provide you with authentic spirituality. However, you are free to choose any of them to help you reach your purpose in life.

3. **When you are spiritual, you see one reality with three distinct universes, physical, mental, and spiritual.** When you are spiritual, where you look to find purpose, meaning, and energy for the trip to Heaven has just increased

4. **Heaven is God's playground.** If we are going to live there...Forever, then we must know how to survive there. Living in a material and spatial world does not prepare us to live in Heaven, spirituality does.

5. **Everything in the physical and mental universe corrupts, that is, matures towards an end.** Yet, the spiritual universe on earth also corrupts because we have evolved from animality and are still not perfect. We commit sin. Sin leads us off the authentic path away from God's energy. Sin is the false god of the golden calf, one whose pleasure and promises are shallow and fleeting. Here is the important part. God gives you the tools to keep you re-centered, once your center drifts, due to sin. This is reconciliation, one of the seven diamonds God gives us to survive imperfection while on the earth.

6. **What is invisible to the eye can be real.** Heaven is invisible, but it is real, nevertheless. Humans don't do well with something they cannot see. This is why we have a problem with Heaven. But wait! If the Kingdom of Heaven lies within you, then you have, right now, everything you need to survive and flourish in Heaven.

7. **Heaven is about choices.** Your center provides you with the correct direction to take. Your journey will be different from mine. Our centers must be the same, but our paths to get there will be different, due to the choices we make. Some of us will never make it to Heaven, due to our choices.

8. **Grace is God's energy overshadowing us.** We can't get to Heaven without it. This is the only energy able to sustain us in Heaven. Like the manna in the desert that sustained the Israelites, and the living bread we eat on earth, this energy allows us to live in pure love...Forever.

9. **Life is all about knowing, loving, and serving God on earth, so that we can continue that relationship in Heaven...Forever.**

> *You make your Heaven,*
> *while you on earth.*

Here are some interesting thoughts.

- √ The Heaven you make while you are here on earth will be the Heaven you live in...Forever.

- √ Heaven is a place where God's shares life with you...Forever. Everything we know about life on earth points to that as being absolutely foolish.

- √ Heaven is a universe where God lives. God wants you to live there. You can't live in the presence of pure energy without some artificial containment area. This is what you make on earth by knowing, loving, and serving God. The purpose of The Master was to glorify the Father. Your purpose is to glorify the Father through the Son, our Master. Read John 17.

- √ If you are spiritual, your choices will reflect it. Every sunrise, all sunsets, the wind on your face, the warm sun on your back as you walk in the garden, the smell of jasmine and orange blossoms, and the sounds of birds in the trees, all may be your Heaven later on, if you glorify the Father through the Son and link every thing authentic to Him. That is why starting the day with a morning offering, giving glory to the Father through the Son, is so important. Every day is a new day.

- √ Only Christ can make all things new, over and over again. Only you can will it be so.

LEARNING POINTS

1. If the purpose is to discover how to know, love, and serve God in this life, you take with you what God values.

2. There are no secret societies, magical conspiracies about the children of Jesus, hidden treasures that have musty scrolls telling that Christianity was an elaborate hoax, and no gospels that tell of the end of the world. You live your life in the context of a community of believers and discover meaning the old-fashioned way. You learn it. If you want to read early writings before there was even a Bible, as we know it, look up *http://www.newadvent.org/fathers/*

3. In Heaven, we will know how everything fits together. Now, we can use our faith, belief, and our reason, to figure it out.

4. If everything you say, do, think and experience in life is to prepare you to live in the next phase of your life, why not look forward to the trip? That is easier said than done. Our lack of faith has our minds questioning, "Why if it is really THE END and not Heaven?"

5 All we can do is hope that the words The Master has given to us are true. Read John 11:25-27. These words must be more than just a reading from Scriptures. They must fuel the passion to live life here on earth to its fullest, so that we can take all of it with us to Heaven.

WHO HELPS YOU GET THERE?

"Even though each and every one of us dies alone, we take with us the sum of what we have learned about what is authentic in life, those lessons we learned about what is false and fickle, and those relationships we have made that are authentic and lasting."

Michael F. Conrad, Ed.D.

An authentic center allows you to have *synergy* with God. An authentic center allows *energy* to flow between God and you. An authentic center allows your three universes to achieve *resonance* with each other...Forever.

You die alone, but
no one goes to Heaven
by themselves.

<u>Here are some ideas to discuss with your friends and colleagues.</u>

√ You are born into this life alone, but through the efforts of your mother and father.

√ You live your life interacting with other people. Along the way, you find out what is worthwhile and what is not. You do not go to Heaven by yourself. Who else can stand by your side?

√ If you are spiritual, and have a spiritual center, then your destination is Heaven, as long as you keep centered. You must discover what is authentic about behaviors and discard all relationships that are poison to your spirit. This is called forgiveness, reconciliation, and a firm purpose of intent to do good.

√ When you die, you move to another level of maturity. This is Heaven. Love lives here. To the extent you have learned to love on earth, you will enjoy it in Heaven.

√ Your mind is a computer that holds all your attempts to find meaning, and seek what is true. Life is a chance to discover meaning. For spiritual persons, this includes living in Heaven...Forever.

Is there more to spirituality than having a personal relationship with The Master?

√ Can there be anything greater than a personal relationship with our Master? That is certainly part of it. Can you think of what else there might be in the plan of salvation? Remember, you are not alone. The spiritual world is not your private county club where you are the only member. Read John 10:6-18.

√ Like marriage, a spiritual relationship with The Master grows as we mature, as least from our perspective.

√ In marriage, couples that the Spirit joins, may have different paths but one source of power. It is so difficult to live with another person and allow them to be independent. Relationship means you become more than one part of the equation. Your part of the equation allows you to help solve it. Read how the gifts of the Spirit help both of your spirits. Galatians 5:22-24.

√ In your spiritual relationship with each other, always seek that which gives you a greater ability to love authentically. In your spiritual relationship with God, know that the purpose of The Master was to give glory to the Father through the Son. Read John 17. Your purpose is to give honor and glory to the Father through the Son. Where can you see these patterns of relationship today?

Name some people who have influenced your journey to... Forever. Why were they so influential?

1. ____

2. ____

3. ____

LEARNING POINTS

1. All of us are headed somewhere. One perspective is that we are just headed for death, then that is all there is. Another way of thinking is that death is only a doorway to another dimension, one we prepare for our whole lives.

2. The doorway is a person who told us that He is the Way, the Truth, and the Life.

3. The best way to get to Heaven is to follow the footprints of The Master. He walked through the minefield of life. So can you. Can you see the footprints?

4. Everything in life is somehow interconnected. Likewise, whatever you do, what you value, your spirituality, the recognition of relationship as the best part of living, all connecting you with Heaven.

5. Far from being a white room with no spatial dimensions against which we can relate, Heaven uses the constructs of our authentic thoughts to build a framework in which we find happiness.

6. The collective wisdom of all humans could not design a heaven. What awaits us in Heaven. Heaven is continuing to live with what we have discovered as meaningful on earth, as long as it is consistent with who God is.

MINING GOLD FOR HEAVEN

"Faith may be a gift, but Heaven is not. For one thing, you must want to go there as your part of your center of life. Another consideration is that it is not easy to get there. Maybe that is how Faith and Hope fits in with Love. To go to Heaven, you must learn to mine, or dig for it. You have heard of mining for gold. You must also mine to reach Heaven. In my book, Three Rules of the Spiritual Universe, I set forth three macro themes that run through human experience. One of them is that you must struggle mightily to keep yourself centered, once you have made a choice to put God as your center. Mining for Heaven is a lifelong endeavor, one that takes a tremendous amount of energy. In addition, where do you think you can get such huge amounts of energy? Not your electric company. The Master gives us all that we need to mine for Heaven. He will not do one thing for us, however, and that is to dig."

Faith is a gift, but one that you can lose by not using it.

Follow the yellow brick road, if you want to mine for a faith home.

Can you imagine mining for gold without the proper tools?

Candice had no idea how to answer her son, when he asked her how he could talk to God. Born an Evangelical Christian, she fell away from her faith after two failed marriages and a series of miserable relationships. As a single mother, she knew she had to provide for the spiritual upbringing of her son, but she lost touch with that side of her being. She happened onto a Catholic Priest in one of her library study groups and started up a conversation. The Priest told her to follow the yellow brick road, if she wanted to get back to her roots. Your roots are those you had when you were young. Start there, he said, and follow it wherever it may lead you. Candice asked him where to start. He looked at her feet and said right here is as good a place as any. He encouraged her to return to the place where she grew up and talk to her pastor. Candice took the Priest's advice and began with her faith home. She was surprised how glad people were to welcome her into her old fellowship. The pastor was new, but she remembered the wonderful feeling she received when worshipping, fellowship afterwards, and the study sessions on the Bible. She took her son, age 14, with her. For three years, Candice attended the church and healed her life. Her journey took a turn when she decided to move to a Lutheran church and change her view of spirituality. The yellow brick road can take any one of us in different directions. Candice's journey is hers to make. She mined for spiritual treasures and found more than she could have imagined. Various denominations helped her on her way, but it was her way.
What tools did she use to mine for spiritual gold?

You must mine to find a personal relationship with God.

There are two dimensions to a personal relationship. One is between you and God, the other one is between you and the body of Christ. You may not believe this way, so be critical when you read this statement.

Alfonso, an Eastern Orthodox Christian, was concerned that his baby boy be baptized as soon as possible. His wife, Cecelia, was Pentecostal and thought that they should wait for baptism until he made a conscious commitment for Christ. Alfonso's family made such a fuss, that Cecelia relented and baptized the baby.

In terms of mining for meaning, both sides were looking at two different dimensions of personal relationship. Unfortunately, they could not see the big picture and process what they were thinking. They had denominational incumbency--the inability to think beyond the boundaries of what THEY THOUGHT their religion taught.

1. If you were a spiritual counselor, engaged by both Alfonso and Cecelia to mediate this crisis in their marriage, what would you say to them to help them gain perspective?

2. How would you approach the subject of baptism so that both traditions could be respected?

3. Will this lead to a dissolution of their marriage?

You must mine to find how to build your Heaven here on earth.

Digging for gold on earth is not easy. By now, you have probably figured out that mining means digging, which takes work. Have you ever panned for gold? In Arkansas, there is a place where you can pay a fee and mine for diamonds.http:*//www.treasurefish.com/arkansas%20metal %20detecting.htm.* You can actually pan for gold in North Carolina.*http://www.geology.enr.state.nc.us/*

Let's say you wanted to pan for gold or dig for diamonds. Do you think you will find them laying on the ground. Maybe, but probably not. The process is what is fun, just like going fishing. You may not catch anything, but it is still enjoyable. If you pan for gold, you must get in a stream and collect dirt from the creek bottom in a pan. Then you swirl it around until you find the gold stuff. Not all gold stuff is real gold. You have to know what is real from what is fool's gold.

In your discussion group, talk about this analogy as it applies to your spirituality.

- If spirituality is just a dead commitment to a center, then should you forget about it?
- Do you have to work for your spirituality to make it constantly renewed? The fact is, over a lifetime of struggling to keep yourself centered, you are not just born again one time, your commitment requires you to be renewed each day. If you don't water your lawn, it will not grow. You are the grass, Faith is the water. All the Faith in the world won't help, if you don't water it.

You must mine to discover how to use God's energy to sustain you in Heaven.

What kind of a God would accept us into Heaven as adopted children and not provide us with what we need to sustain us there? Heaven is God's playground, not ours. When we die, we can take with us only those values and experiences that are authentic. How do we know what is authentic? We must dig for it. Here are some of the riches we must mine.

- √ God gave us the Ten Commandments to teach us principles (Deuteronomy 5); Remember I am using the New Jerusalem Bible.
- √ God gave us his only begotten Son (Philippians 2:5-12)
- √ The Master, God's Son, gave us the Beatitudes to guide us not only how to live now, but to prepare us for Heaven (Matthew 5)
- √ God told us that we must decrease, while The Master must increase (Philippians 38-18);
- √ The Master told us that anyone who believes in Him, even if he dies, will live, and whoever lives and believes in Him will never die (John 11:25-27);
- √ The Master said we must be born of water and the spirit (John 3:3-5);
- √ The Master asks us to carry the burden of our life, but not without His help (Matthew 11:28-30).

You need all of these principles of life to get to Heaven. The ironic thing is they contain a lifetime of wisdom and applications. They are so deep and life sustaining, that you never quite understand what they mean. Heaven is just a continuation of these principles...Forever. Make sure you have the correct ones.

> *You must mine the riches of human relationship to find out what is authentic.*

Do you think that sustaining any type of human relationship comes without a price? The question is, are you willing to pay it?

Derrick and Lori were sweethearts from their time together in Elementary School. Never apart, they grew up together and were natural companions that complimented each other in every way. When they got married, no one was surprised. Lori settled in to be a homemaker, while Derrick was the coach for a local high school football team. Derrick's work took him on the road for long periods of time, scouting teams, practice after school hours, and team games on the road. Both deeply spiritual, Derrick and Lori attended a Marriage Encounter weekend. *http://www.marriage- encounter.org/* They renewed their commitment to each other, especially in the context of their relationship with God. What both Derrick and Lori learned from their weekend recollection was how to put the long periods of Derrick's absence in perspective, God's perspective. They did not have to like the long separation, but there were several ways they could sustain each other in good times and in bad, in sickness

Write down three spiritual principles that you would use to gain perspective in your relationship, in times of duress and stress?

> *You must discover that only the rich get to Heaven, but that you must use God's riches, not yours.*

What is your purpose in life? You can be the most successful executive, a woman who is at the top of her chosen field, or children who are making straight A's in school and headed for a bright future, but if you do not know your purpose in life, all of this is for naught. Read Matthew 22: 34-40. A self-audit will allow you to re-discover your center.

1. Heaven in God's playground. If you want to play there, you must use His rules. Do you know what those are? Read Galatians 5:16-26.

2. As a spiritual person, you have special powers to see ordinary things in the physical and mental universes, and link them with God's purpose. Do you know how to see reality from the perspective of The Master? Read Philippians 2:2-12.

3. The Master came to earth with a mission. Do you know what that purpose was? If you do, and you adopt it, you align yourself with pure energy, pure love, and pure service. If that was not enough, your alignment produces the energy you need to sustain you in this life, and to fulfill you in the next. Read John 17:11-26.

4. That in all things, God be glorified. Read I Peter 4:11.

LEARNING POINTS

1. You must discover who you are. Who you are is based not only on where you have been, but also on where you want to go. Perspective provides you with the ability to see in the future.

2. The Master has given us the means to reach our destiny. He will not walk it for you, but He will walk with you, if you have the spiritual awareness to see.

3. God created all that you see, all that will be, so that everyone has a chance to get to Heaven. Not everyone believes in this way.

4. Only the rich get to Heaven, and only those who are in sync with God's energy, can make it to a place of sustained happiness. Without God's help as the great Enabler, His energy would burn out your mental circuits and fry your mind.

5. Mining for wealth is a preoccupation on earth. Mining for Heaven should be your aim. It is there that true riches reside. Not all make it to that level of reality.

6. For you to be authentic, your center must reflect the reality in Heaven.

7. Mining takes work. God will not dig for you, but with you.

SUSTAINING YOUR CENTER

"Now that you have chosen a center that is authentic comes the hard part. You must keep it centered. Centers drift like the tide, due to the fact that we live in a world that can't stand a center of unconditional love."

The Center for Contemplative Practice

Once you are spiritual, you are a pilgrim in a foreign land.

It is not enough for you to go to church every Sunday and pray for forgiveness and strength. Today's prayers do not help tomorrow's challenges. Each and every day, you must begin with a Morning Offering, a rebirth, a recommitment to living one-day-at-a-time. you must offer all things in, with, and through The Master to the Father. It only takes a moment at the beginning of each day, but what an important moment that is.

If you are a pilgrim in a foreign land, here are some helps to sustain you and keep you centered. It is important that you link what you do to give glory to The Father through The Son.

1. BE A VISIBLE MEMBER OF THE BODY OF THE MASTER. The Master lives through you. You must worry that, whatever you do, it is worthy of the trust that The Master has placed in you.

2. EVERY DAY, LINK YOUR LIFE WITH GOD'S. Your spirituality must be from God, not from within you, or from merely human values.

3. THINK SPIRITUAL! Your center is under constant pressure to put something unauthentic there. You might say, the default for humans is to be animal, not spiritual. Why else are you constantly pulled in the direction of self-indulgence? Read Galatians 5:16-26. Read my book, Spiritual Apes: The Struggle To Be Spiritual, Vol. III, for an in-depth treatment of this struggle.

> *Be a visible member of the body of The Master.*

Use your time on earth is to prepare you for the trip to...Forever. Mother lionesses teach their cubs by allowing them to watch them, then hunt with the pack, then make kills on their own. Humans have something that lion cubs do not. They are free to choose anything they want as their center.

Janice and Roy were not very good church go-ers. They loved the good life, good food, good vacations, good friends, good hobbies, good drinking, and good sex. Their center not only revolved, they had no idea what to put there. They were not worried about the next life, being so busy enjoying this one. They had all the blessings this life could bestow. Janice was a nurse, and Roy was a principle at a local high school. They had no children. They said they believed in a higher form of being, a God, but became confused about spirituality after that. They were not worry about it. They were the center of their own lives. Life was good for Janice and Roy.

Janice and Roy's best friend, Duane, and his wife Candice, were almost the polar opposite of them. Duane and Candice were very good church go-ers, although they would tell you that they were members of the body of The Master. Their faith was the center of their life. Their relationship with The Master gave them an anchor, and also a center. They had four children, whom they instilled with their love of life. Life was good to Duane and Candice.

Two different couples with different centers. What was the difference?

> *Faith is a gift, but one you must cultivate daily.*

Faith is a gift from God, but it is a gift you must appreciate, and one that takes cultivation. Daily!

- Once you have an authentic center, you will spend your whole life trying to keep it there.

- We are in daily need of salvation, redemption. Daily! Not everyone believes these ideas. Be critical and look for the assumptions underlying them. Some religions think that salvation is automatic with acceptance of The Master. Others think that once you accept The Master, the struggle to keep your center authentic just begins. What do you think is consistent with what you know about life?

- Why would we have to forgive others, if we were on the conveyor belt of automatic entrance to Heaven? This is one principle of the Reformation that separates how people think about salvation. What do you believe and why?

- If you are alcoholic, how do you stay sober? Daily! If you are drug dependent, how do you remain free? Daily!

- If you are a human being who has chosen an authentic center, how do you keep from slipping back into sinfulness? Daily!

- Who gives you that strength? Read Matthew 11:28-30.

THINK SPIRITUALLY!

Over a Starbuck's Grande, Elaine and Jean would often talk of their latest sexual conquests. On this day, for some reason, their talk brushed on religion. Elaine considered herself a non-believer. She told Jean that she could never belong to an organized religion. Jean would tease her back, saying that her only other option was an unorganized one. One thing was evident from this conversation. How could two friends be so compatible with boyfriends, work, politics, and relationships, yet be so radically different?

Two years earlier, Jean joined a charismatic faith community, which suited what she was looking for in her life. The people were caring, non-judgmental, respectful of her slightly divergent beliefs, and non-dogmatic about their church. Elaine had vastly different experiences, ones that led her to reject anything to do with religion as so much hypocrisy. Both Elaine and Jean met monthly to feed the homeless at a local shelter that cared for families. They were both caring and inspiring advocates for battered women and hosted many fund raisers for their favorite charity. At work, both women were models for leadership and change in the organization. Their many talents were evident in how they developed several programs to help pets and pet owners during a hurricane or tornado. Life was very good to both women. One woman was spiritual, while one was not. What was the difference between the two? Is there a difference? Certainly, both women felt they had a full and vigorous life, one of fulfillment and meaning. What difference does spirituality make in the life of Jean? Does she have something that Elaine does not have? What is it?

LEARNING POINTS

1. Your center should be outside of you, so the energy with which you sustain it must also come from another universe.

2. Having a center is not the same as having a center that will propel you to Heaven. Having a center is not the same as having a center that will sustain you in this life and through the next.

3. God's energy sustains you in the spiritual universe, both in this life and the next. The question is do you know how to tap into that energy?

4. There are two dimensions to spiritual relationship: your relationship with God, and your relationship with others.

5. If your car is due for a scheduled maintenance, where do you take it? Where do you go for the 40-year checkup on your spiritual motor?

6. Once you accept that you are in God's playground, you must continue to work to keep yourself there. God does not change, but you can drift into unauthentic ways of thinking and doing, if you are not careful. Read about the true disciple in Matthew 7:21-27.

FIFTY TABLE-TOP DISCUSSION POINTS

HOW TO USE THESE DISCUSSION POINTS

Here are fifty (50) final points you can use in a tabletop discussion about spirituality and faith. There are at least two ways you can arrange people to learn. You may wish to use these discussions in a tabletop adult learning meeting; one question discussed and reported out by all the tables, which is a more in-depth approach. On the other hand, you can give a different question to a different table, thus having more ideas from multiple viewpoints. Make sure you read the Scripture texts.

1. Why is it important to have a Center? What have you selected as your Center? Did you analyze it?

2. What makes your center authentic? Is there such a thing as a bad center? Give some examples.

3. Is your center correct because you hold it, or do you hold it because it is correct? Why are there so many different centers? Who is to say which one is correct?

4. How can someone who is not spiritual have an authentic center? Can this person go to Heaven?

5. Is there a difference between religion and denomination? How does your freedom to choose enter into spirituality?

6. Name some false centers. Why are they false? Who says so?

7. What does freedom to choose have to do with selecting a center? If there is but one truth, why are there so many different interpretations of it? How can people differ in their beliefs yet be similar in their faith? John 3:11-21.

8. Being spiritual is a free act of the will. How can different people choose to believe radically different faith systems? Read John 8:30-32

9. Your purpose is to find the correct center that leads you to the Kingdom of Heaven. What have you chosen as your center? Read John 15:1-17.

10. What does the template of the Trinity, one reality with three distinct persons, have to do with three distinct universes, physical, mental, and spiritual, yet one reality? When you are spiritual, where do you look to find purpose, meaning, and energy for the trip?

11. Heaven is God's playground. If we are going to live there...Forever, then we must know how to survive there. What does your Heaven look like? Read John 14:9-21.

12. How does spirituality prepare you to live in a dimension without any material frame of reference? Will we get spiritual claustrophobia? Read John 14:1-4.

13. Everything in the physical and mental universe corrupts, that is, matures towards an end. In Heaven, there is no end of anything...Forever. How will you be able to withstand those dimensions? How can you live in a place of 100% perfection, while you are imperfect? Read John 6:34-40.

14. What is invisible to the eye can be real. Heaven is invisible, but it is real nevertheless. If the Kingdom of Heaven lies within you, then what does your Heaven look like right now?

15. Grace is God's energy sustaining us. We can't get to Heaven without it. This is the only energy able to sustain us in Heaven. How does that happen? Read John 14:23-31.

16. Life is all about knowing, loving, and serving God on earth, so that we can continue that relationship in Heaven...Forever. How does relationship happen in Heaven? Is there pleasure? Is there pain? Do you pay taxes? If achieving relationships is the key to getting to Heaven, what will that relationship with God look like? Read John 4.

17. Heaven is about choices. Your center provides you with the correct direction to take. Your journey will be different from mine. How can we make it to Heaven, when all our paths are different? What is the one constant that we must use to sustain ourselves in Heaven? Read John 14:5-7

18. Our centers must be the same, but our paths to get there will bc different, due to the choices we make. Some of us will never make it to Heaven, due to our choices. What does the resurrection have to do with choice of centers? Read John 11:17-27.

19. If you have a center, what was The Master's center? Read John 17.

20. Why must you dig for spiritual gold? Isn't faith a gift? Why would you have to work for something you already have? Why is stewardship important to sustain your center? Read Matthew 16:24-28.

21. Why is forgiveness necessary for someone wanting to live 100% of their human capacity in Heaven? Is there forgiveness in Heaven, after you die? Why or why not?

22. What are your assumptions about faith? Is faith an automatic pass to Heaven, no matter what you do or say that is false and sinful? Is faith like a credit card from Best Buys that lets you charge items that you must later on pay? When is faith not enough? Who has authority to say what is true and authentic? Read Matthew 7:21-29.

23. Why is power a false center? Who says so? Read Matthew 20:24-28.

24. Write a parable, using examples you experienced this week, to describe a false sense of power. Read Matthew 4.

25. What are the tools you can use to mine for Heavenly gold in this life? Read Matthew 5.

26. How do you sustain or keep centered, in the midst of this world's temptations? What is difficult to do with mere human help, is possible with God's grace. Read Matthew 11:28-30.

27. Why is being rich a temptation to keep from centering yourself on what is authentic? Read Matthew 6:19-21.

28. When you believe in what your denomination says is true, are all beliefs equal? Are some beliefs more central to the core message of The Master than others? Who determines that? Read John 14:10-21.

29. Once you have discovered the center of your life, you will spend the rest of your life trying to keep yourself centered on what you have selected. Who helps you? Read John 15.

30. Why are drugs, alcohol, and orgiastic sex centers that will make you feel good, but will not last...Forever? What will? Read I Corinthians 13.

31. Have each person write down the purpose of their lives. Share these ideas with your group. What deductions can you draw from listening to the various purposes? Read John 3:16.

32. When you are born of water and the spirit, is do you just give up and get on the conveyor belt of life? Read John 3:4-8. Is there more to life? What is it?

33. Write down the meaning of the word "forgiveness." Why is this act of contrition so important to your spirituality. What does "forgiveness" have to do with keeping centered? Matthew 18:21-22.

34. If you have the Scriptures, why do you need a church to tell you what it means? Read John 10:6-18.

35. What is the one center of your church? Does it both nourish you, the individual, and you, the body of The Master? Read John 6:34-40.

36. How can individuals in the church be sinful, yet the body of The Master, the church, be holy? Read John 17:1-26.

37. What does belonging to a faith home have to do with sustaining your center, while you are in this world? What can a faith support system do for you? What can you do for it? Read John 8:12. What does the light of life mean, in terms of your center?

38. If your center gives you energy to sustain you, how often must you touch your center to renew it? Read John 6:52-58.

39. Is your center consistent with the gifts of the spirit? How can seemingly good people do bad things? Read Galatians 5:16-26.

40. What is the link between Adam and The Master? Do you see any parallels? Read Romans 5:12-21.

41. How can you begin to make your Heaven while you are still on this earth? Read Luke 7:21.

42. Who helps you get to Heaven? List five persons who can help you get to Heaven. Why did you choose these people?

43. What control do you have over people that disagree with your view of spirituality? Are you the center of what is true and righteous about spiritual? What is the danger of thinking that you are god? Read Deuteronomy 6:14-25.

44. Name five ways people can put themselves as center of spirituality for everyone, making themselves into god. What is the danger of this? Read John 8:21-29.

45. What does it mean to be free from the law of sin and death? Read Romans 8:1-17. How does sin keep you from receiving grace, even though you have faith?

46. What sustains you, when the winds of disbelief swirl around you and cloud your direction? Read John 16:32-32.

47. What is your personal faith in The Master? Into what context does this faith fit? Do you have faith without context? Read Matthew 18:15-18 and Acts 15:7-12.

48. Every religion has a particular way to look at their center? What is the center of your religion?

49. You are destined for Heaven. How can you get there? Read John 14:1-4

50. Write down what you know about the following themes. Discuss these themes with each other. What do you notice about what people think about the topic?

What must you believe to go to Heaven? ________________

What is Church and why is it important to help you get to Heaven? ________________

Is your Church like the Kentucky Derby, a place where people go to show off their best hats and fashions? If not, where does it fit?

What sustains you in time of crisis? How do you resolve spiritual disputes? ________________

May you have wisdom to discern
authentic from false centers, to walk
the path of enlightenment with friends,
rather than alone,
and so find your purpose for life.

May your search for meaning
allow you to discover the
Kingdom of Heaven
within you.

May you have,
in your minds and
in your hearts,
the Grace and Peace
of Our Father, that of
Our Lord and Master,
Jesus Christ,
with the Spirit of Truth.

May we be together
one day...Forever.

The Center for Contemplative Practice is a ministry of people devoted to providing spiritual resources for adults, such as publishing books, retreats, training, blogs, and on-line meditations.

DISCLAIMER

The ideas and meditations contained in any books or blogs shared by The Center for Contemplative Practice do not represent the official, authoritative teaching of the Roman Catholic Church or any Cistercian Monastery or Lay Cistercian group. These ideas and are the results of *lectio divina* spiritual meditations by the author and reflect only his interpretation of Catholic spiritual thoughts through contemplation.

ABOUT THE AUTHOR

Michael F. Conrad, B.S., M.R.E., Ed.D., retired from a full life of trying to make money, seek fame and recognition by the world, all without much success. Coming to his senses, even after the age of 70, he now struggles to have in him the mind of Christ Jesus. (Philippians 2:5-12) Still running the race and searching for the prize, he has had a lifetime of activities to help him in his quest: he is proud to have been a U.S. Army Chaplain, pastor of parish ministry, adjunct instructor of Adult Education at Indiana University (Bloomington) and University of South Florida (Tampa) and Barry University (Florida), high school instructor of religion, trainer of managers and supervisors, adjunct trainer for the Florida Certified Public Manager program, instructional designer for the State of Florida, former Florida Supreme Court Certified Family Mediator, and currently a publisher, blogger and author, He is a Lay Cistercian member of Our Lady of the Holy Spirit Monastery, Conyers, Georgia, proud father of a daughter, and a humbled husband.

CONTEMPLATIVE PRACTICE SERIES

SPIRITUAL APES: Our Journey to Forever, Volume I

SPIRITUAL APES: Our Journey from Animality to Spirituality, Volume II

SPIRITUAL APES: Our Struggle to Be Spiritual, Volume III

HOW TO GRIEVE WELL. What Happens to You When You Have Lost a Loved One? Spirituality for the Bereaved

What Happens to You When You Have Lost a Pet? Spirituality for Pet Owners

HOW TO DIE WELL. So You Know You Are Going to Die, Now What? A Spiritual Preparation for Life ...Forever

Searching for Love in the Garden of Eden: Spirituality for the Lonely of Heart

If Life is a Journey, Have You Lost the Road Map? Spiritual Toolkit for Divorced Men

The Three Rules of the Spiritual Universe: Choose An Authentic Center that Leads to Heaven.

You Are My Heritage: A Father Thoughts to His Daughter as She Enters College

17 Skills Moms and Dads Must Teach Their Children: Show Your Children How to Get to Heaven

Legally Married, Mentally and Spiritually Divorced: Refreshing Tired Relationships.

Have You Lost All Your Marbles, or Just Your EX? Spirituality for Divorced Women

Who Does God Think He Is, Anyway? Guidance from the Master

The Woman Who Changed Time: Spirituality and Time

Who Rows Your Boat? How You Can Be Happier Than You Can Possibly Imagine

How Moms and Dads Can Be Spiritual Directors for their Children: Developmental Spirituality

Is Your Spiritual Life Running on Empty? Overcoming Spiritual Depression

JOURNAL OF MEANING SERIES

Come, Share Your Lord's Joy: A Journal to Prepare for Life... Forever.

You Are My Heritage: Thoughts on How Much You Mean to Me

Spiritual Estate Planning: Spiritual Wealth Building.

The Center of My Life: Thoughts About the Assumptions Underlying What I Believe

LAZER LEARNING SERIES

Mining for Heavenly Gold While On Earth: How To Center Yourself On What Is Authentic

How to Stop Assumicide: How to Think Critically About What You Believe, Without Destroying Your Faith

Five Steps to Build a Better Future for Your Community

Resolving Spiritual Conflicts: Spirituality for Split-Religion Moms and Dads

Websites of Note

Here are some wonderful, contemplative websites in which you may find some rest for your soul.

- *http://www.trappist.net*
- *http//www.verbum.com*
- *http://www.biblegateway.com/cgi-bin/bible*
- *http://www.universalis.com/lauds.htm*
- *http://www.christianmystics.com/*
- *http://http://www.glencairnabbey.org*
- *http://www.catholic.net/RCC/Indices/*
- *http: www.carlmccolman.com*
- *http://www.laycisterciansofgethsemane.org*
- *http://www.cistercianpublications.org*
- *http://www.bible-researcher.com/new- Jerusalem-bible. html*
- *http://www.centeringprayer.com/cntrgpryr.htm*
- *http://www.monk.org*
- *http://www.newadvent.com*
- *http://www.ewtn.com/library/PRIESTS/BENRULE.*
- *www.scotthahn.com*

THE FINAL IMPERATIVES

LISTEN TO ME, FOR I AM MEEK AND HUMBLE OF HEART. Matthew 11:28-30

√ **Thirsty? Drink of the living waters! John 7:37.**

√ **Hungry? Eat the food that gives eternal life! John 6:33-38.**

√ **Bewildered? Believe in the Master! John 3:11-21.**

√ **Without hope? Be not afraid! John 13:33-35.**

√ **Lost? Find the way! John 14:6-7.**

√ **Tired because of the pain? Be renewed! John 15:1-7.**

√ **Afraid to die? Find peace! John 14:1-4.**

√ **Afraid to believe? Believe! John 11:25-27.**

√ **Without a family? Listen! John 10:7-18.**

√ **In darkness? Walk in the light! John 8:12.**

√ **Spiritually depressed? Be healed! John 5:24**

Welcome, good and faithful servant, into the Kingdom prepared for you before the world began.

Write your center in the space above.

MORNING OFFERING

Father, through your Son, our Master, you have given us the Way, the Truth, and the Life.

As I go out into this fresh day, may whatever I say, whatever I do, all my thoughts and intentions, be offered to your praise and glory. That in all things today, may you be glorified.

www.thelearningdoctor.com

CONTEMPLATIVE REFLECTIONS

Readings for CONTEMPLATION as you humbly kneel before the Most Blessed Sacrament of the Altar in Eucharistic Adoration.

I order you, O Sleeper, to awake!
I did not create you to be held a prisoner in hell.
Rise from the dead, for I am the life of the dead.
Rise up, work of my hands, you were created in my image.
Rise, let us leave this place, for you are in me and I am in you.
Together, we form only one person and we cannot be separated.

--From an Ancient Homily on Holy Saturday, Easter Eve

There is a thread you follow. It goes among
Things that change, But it doesn't change.
People wonder about what you are pursuing.
You have to explain about the thread.
But it is hard for others to see.
While you hold it, you can't get lost.
Tragedies happen; people get hurt or die; and you suffer and get old.

Nothing you do can stop time's unfolding.
You don't ever let go of the thread.

--William Stafford, "The Way It is."

That in all things,
God may be glorified.

-- Rule of St. Benedict

Energy travels at the speed of light.

Throughout your whole life,
with all its opportunities, with
all its disappointments,
you can only travel at the
speed of enlightenment.

--The Center for
Contemplative Practice

THE STRUGGLE TO BE SPIRITUAL

Hidden waves of life flush over my spirit,
every day, the tide of life nourishes me,
the life-giving nutrients are there for my taking.

All I need do is lift my head from the physical
work and see with the eyes of The Master.

Just the slightest nod each morning links me
with pure energy, the source of all that lives,
here, and throughout the universe.

The key of my survival lies in my ability to
discern the purpose of life and join myself with
that God's meaning. Life's struggles are endless
but so is the energy of The Master.

The Center for Contemplative Practice

www.ingramcontent.com/pod-product-compliance
Lightning Source LLC
Chambersburg PA
CBHW060659030426
42337CB00017B/2688

* 9 7 8 1 9 3 0 3 0 1 6 3 4 *